#TEAMWORK **tweet**

140 Powerful Bite-Sized Insights on Lessons for Leading

Teams to Success

By Caroline G. Nicholl
Foreword by Rafael Pastor

First Printing: July 2010

Paperback ISBN: 978-1-61699-030-5 (1-61699-030-9)

eBook ISBN: 978-1-61699-031-2 (1-61699-031-7)

Place of Publication: Silicon Valley, California, USA

Paperback Library of Congress Number: 2010926199

Advance Praise

"Caroline Nicholl's provocative book on teams guides us to be change-ready and to reinvent ourselves on an ongoing basis. Recognizing that teams achieve more than any individual can and are vital to business success, Nicholl explains the one golden rule: It takes an effective leader to realize the full potential of each team and marshal it to successful outcomes."

Rafael Pastor, CEO and Chairman of the Board, Vistage International

---

"Caroline's work on teams is highly relevant, particularly in a tough economy: her insightful work with one of our divisional teams surfaced issues that clarified exactly the priorities the team needed to address to increase its performance in a way that the team could hear. The team quickly got motivated to action. Caroline's approach is practical, sensitive and to the point, precipitating rapid learning and improvement."

Jay Reid, Senior Vice President, Labor Ready Inc.

"Caroline Nicholl has tackled a familiar topic with an unusual twist: her tweets on teams are thought-provoking and will help any team build awareness of its strengths and performance gaps. Her work with Anybill catapulted my team to a different level of action. Her acumen and business sense are spot on."

Matt Voorhees, President & CEO, Anybill Inc.

"TEAMWORK tweet is a clear guide for anyone who works in or with teams: Caroline's emphasis on leadership and team process is not for the timid. Her timely book reminds us why teams are important and the critical role a leader plays to tap into a team's power. Teamwork is a common phenomenon but Caroline's work on teams is a rare gift."

Ken Crerar, President, Council of Insurance Agents and Brokers

---

"Caroline's insights shift one's thinking ... a powerful coach for anyone or any team trying to make needed change, she listens at a level you are not immediately aware of until, bingo! You see a clear path toward change. Her coaching is purposeful and makes a big impact."

Elisabeth Hayes, Executive Coaching client

Dedication

To leaders and teams who refuse to approach teamwork casually. Your tough efforts are often misunderstood and deserve broader recognition.

Acknowledgments

Thank you reader: I hope you find concrete take-aways to improve your own team and to advance the world into becoming more humane.

Thanks to those I've ever teamed with. If I knew then what I know now, I'd have been more of a team player; certainly a better team leader.

In particular, thanks to my former colleagues in policing. Cops know good teamwork calls for candor, camaraderie and mutual accountability.

Thanks to all my clients who have given me valuable opportunities to learn the importance of teamwork to the business world and beyond.

Thank you to Rajesh Setty (@*UpbeatNow*) and Tom Batchelder (tom@perficiency.com) who encouraged me to write about teamwork for twitter.

Thanks to the staff at The Broadmoor and CIAB: a fall weekend gig allowed me to tuck myself away with my Acer and to tweet away on teams.

Thanks to Jean Card (jeaniecard@yahoo.com) who gave me her valuable insights and feedback on twittering and is a fab editor.

Thank you to my family and friends in Europe, the US and elsewhere who have helped shape the person I am today, and what I might yet become.

Finally, thanks to Kathy Davis: we've learned much from one another and make a good team.

Why Did I Write This Book?

The way we think about teamwork is outdated. Just as institutions and organizations need reinvention in our changing world, so do teams.

A model clarifying the intersection between leadership, change and teamwork is overdue: it's not only political gridlock we need to overcome.

With today's challenges and data overload, there is no such thing as one leader any more: the full potential of teamwork needs leveraging.

The 'new' economy calls for reexamining the way time, energy and money are used, and to what end, through new teamwork, not old autocracy.

We need well-led, highly-disciplined teamwork focused on world realities. A by-product would be that we all become wiser and more tolerant.

The power of teamwork lies in learning from different people's perspectives, and pooling resources: pulling together, not pulling apart.

I've been on many teams: from building a treehouse with my schoolmate to helping Iraq get back on its feet post – shock 'n awe.

I've had the too rare, good fortune of working on a high performing team. The experience was transforming, and still influences me.

I've known teams that never gelled or fulfilled their promise: teamwork thwarted by weak leadership, poor focus and team trauma.

Team trauma is heart breaking: unresolved conflict and animosity precipitating demoralized staff, chronic insomnia or illness.

In particular, I've learned that great teams need extraordinary leadership involving shared vision, mutual trust and equal resoluteness.

Leaders need to understand they no longer rule. Their humility is required to ensure teams fly high, giving real teamwork a chance.

The lost potential of teams is disheartening if one thinks of the challenges we face and the powerful force of high performing teamwork.

Great teamwork produces amazing outcomes—for team members individually, other stakeholders and beyond: we need more of this.

Bottom line—the world would be far better off if we had more high performing teamwork. The workforce would become more eager too.

I hope this book contributes to a better understanding of how vital teams are, and how vitality now could make all the difference in the world.

140 Powerful Bite-Sized Insights on Lessons for Leading Teams to Success

Contents

Foreword by Rafael Pastor

"'TEAMWORK tweet' reminds leaders to unite high-performing teams with idea generation and rapid collaboration, afforded more so by social media."

Rafael Pastor, CEO and Chairman of the Board, Vistage International

Introduction

Too many teams struggle with underperformance, tension and trauma. Some achieve nothing at all except cynicism and fatigue.

We read a lot about 'gutsy' leaders: dominant characters pulling off some event or overcoming a challenge. This is only half the story.

Even POTUS, the most powerful man in the world, can't pull off change without nimble teamwork.

We need a new model of working: leaders of high-performing teams to effect change without wasting time, money and other resources.

Global and local challenges require us to pool ideas and efforts efficiently and effectively: good teamwork is now a *necessity*.

Organizations and leaders need reminding of the raison d'être for teams: teams have the capacity to think and act better than individuals.

Teams can deal with complexity and produce faster results. Teams can multiply the courage of a single leader in making change happen—and making the change stick.

Too many leaders are ambivalent toward teams. They either avoid their team-building responsibilities or collude with poor teamwork.

Some leaders struggle with teamwork because teams require a *compelling* purpose, *effective* communication and *healthy* conflict.

Most of us are familiar with teams, having experienced them in some shape or form. 75% of organizational life is organized around teams.

Familiarity is perhaps our No. 1 enemy. Be it complacency, denial or clumsy kumbaya efforts at "teambuilding," many teams are failing.

Twenty-one centuries after the birth of a team leader with 12 disciples you might expect the human race to conduct teamwork with adroitness.

What the next twenty-one centuries bring will be shaped for better or worse by teamwork.

I hope this book will spread awareness about team leadership and teams, helping to drive teamwork in the right direction.

If this sounds ambitious, I make no apologies: ambition and teamwork are compatible concepts.

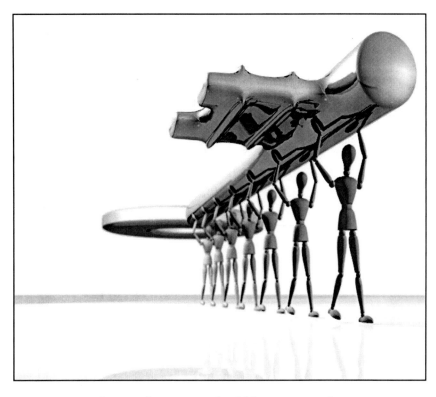

The puzzle pieces to build hot teamwork!

Section I
Why Teamwork Matters Now More Than Ever

The complexity of challenges in our global economy means that we need leaders who can support innovation, collaboration and adaptability. Leaders must be able to harness the real power of teamwork. Today, teamwork, and leadership that can support it, matter more than ever before.

1

The world is changing fast; resources are finite. Traditional sources of leadership have yet to grasp that the way ahead is teamwork.

2

We are global with a capital G. The world is no longer responsive to old systems of power: we need *shared* power and responsibility.

3

The 21st century needs well-led, highly disciplined teamwork focused on current (not old) realities, with the future reality in sight.

4

Teams are as old as the hills but we need a new understanding of their power. Solutions need acceleration that only teamwork delivers.

5

Teamwork is required to address violence, corruption, climate change, wealth disparity, 'peak' oil and water shortages and more.

6

Done right, teamwork can address challenges and opportunities by tapping diverse views, know-how and ideas, mindful that we can all win.

7

Many teams are besieged by underperformance, stress and under-achievement: the current cost is huge; the lost opportunity unfathomable.

8

Teams can offset narrow-minded, prejudiced concerns and self-interest for the greater good. We need the greater good more than ever.

9

Traditional *them versus us* attitudes cause much pain and needless mess. Greed and selfishness have had their day. Ego needs containment.

10

The *delivery* of solutions and new outcomes depend on teamwork. Leadership matters but it will be teamwork that defines true success.

11

We don't need leaders if they're not bringing change: we need more leaders who know innovation is vital and best conducted in teams.

12

The word "team" comes from an old Dutch word *toomk*, meaning to pull together (not pull apart). Let's build a future we can be proud of.

Amplify performance through top notch teamwork

Section II

What, Exactly, Is an Effective Team?

The factors that make a team successful are complex and diverse. Mutual trust, good communication, effective conflict management and clear decision-making each have a role to play. In a successful team, members take away learning and develop skills to combat future challenges.

13

A common definition of a team is 'two or more people working together to achieve a common purpose no single person can achieve alone.'

14

Teams exist to produce **results**. Not to sing Kumbaya or play tiddlywinks. Their rationale is not togetherness for togetherness' sake.

15

No need for a team without goals to achieve. Teams are about **performance**: the sum of the collective efforts of the members.

16

Teams should be tasked with a clear **mission**: robust enough to be a game changer, giving the team a shared sense of purpose and drive.

17

A high-performing team is one where there's mission focus and outcome achievement through mutual support, leadership and diversity.

18

Some leaders are unclear about the value of teams, having never been on a high-performing team: they often overrely on technology.

19

While technology dominates much of our lives these days, let's not forget that well-led teamwork is also a change-maker.

20

Teams are about **people**: teams may require technology but thoughtful leadership is more critical to team performance than is realized.

21

Teams involve people **learning** from, and helping, each other to make decisions and take action to translate vision into reality.

22

Teams can bring a return beyond the mission: members acquire learning and new skills for the organization, their own future and the world.

23

Leaders need to ensure the team has clear goals so its energy is focused. Energy includes team dialogue, feedback, learning and action.

24

Leaders have a role to pave the way for team success: including modeling the behaviors they want from team members.

25

Never underestimate the results a team can achieve. Teams are capable of achieving better and faster results than individuals can achieve by themselves.

26

Teams share information, knowledge and perspectives that minimize blind spots, errors, the impractical, waste and endless daydreaming.

27

Too many leaders convene 'loosey-goosey' teams simply to check up on what their staff are doing. Teams cost money and you need an ROI.

28

Team members need a compelling vision—beyond simple financial goals—to spur meaningful cooperation and to leverage all their talent.

29

Organizations should exist to solve problems, not just make profit for a few. Effective teamwork should lead to more common good.

30

Expectations of teams are frequently too low or focused simply on the bottom line. In turn, members have low hopes for teamwork.

31

Think big—a team needs to have passion around something *important*. Teams need audacious goals that are inspiring and motivating.

32

Over-focus on money and you miss the point of teams: teams can pull off amazing results. Be bold in what you ask and expect of them.

33

Teamwork is about **mutuality**. Members need each other to deliver on the mission. This is difficult for control freaks and narcissists.

34

Teams are about collaborating, cooperating and sharing thoughts and ideas in the context of effective interpersonal relationships.

35

A team is much more than the sum of its parts: the whole takes time to mobilize but the results can be immensely powerful.

36

It is a team's full energy that makes each team special, influential and productive, and why attention to a team's make-up is vital.

37

Just as a cake with one ingredient does not make a very interesting cake, teams should be rich with **diversity**.

38

There's nothing wrong with eggs,
flour and sugar of themselves.
It's just that the mix is full of
possibilities. It's the same with teams.

39

Diversity means pooling people
(toom) with different ages, gender,
knowledge, competencies, opinions,
experiences and styles.

40

You want powerful analysis and problem solving, not *groupthink*. Make the team a good mix of perspectives, experience and knowledge.

41

Pull together people for their diverse skills and potential learning, not for personality characteristics alone.

42

Assemble complementary skills in a team: too many eggs and not enough flour creates a mess. Your talent needs to get along.

43

Teams have a dynamic
and reputation
influenced by several
critical ingredients:
people, leadership,
big mission and
farsightedness.

44

Think performance and far beyond. Done right, a team will achieve something significant *and* the organization and world will gain significantly.

45

Be clear about the difference
between a team accomplishing
significant change and a group
supporting the bureaucracy.

46

Ask: What **mission** needs to be met?
Can a **team achieve this better or
faster? What mix of people** need to
be **pooled** to **work together**?

47

With teams, think big, think mix, think people. Achieve a mission unachievable alone or with identical twins!

Section III

Effective Teamwork Does Not Come out of Thin Air

Effective teamwork does not just happen. Team members must be carefully selected for their diverse skills and knowledge and be given a chance to understand their mission and build a sense of common purpose. When leadership creates the right environment, the team learns how to operate to its full potential, in some cases exceeding all expectations.

48

The key ingredients—people, mission, diversity—of an effective team are one thing: actually pulling them together is another.

49

You can't make a glorious cake simply throwing ingredients together: there has to be intentionality. It's the same with a team.

50

An effective team emerges from paying attention to both *task* and *process*. Stick with me here and you'll prevent an awful lot of trouble.

51

The best teams spend time learning how to be a team: never minimize the importance of trust building, building understanding and bonding.

52

The key *task* is getting—and keeping—the team focused. Imagine baking a cake with your back to the mixing bowl.

53

A business team that is focused on its purpose is like a sports team focused on winning.

54

Ask any team to explain its focus and you will be surprised by a remarkable consensus or total disagreement. Seldom is it in between.

55

A team has focus or it is all-over-the-place, meaning meetings for meetings' sake, sipping lattes, gossiping, whining... you get the gist.

56

Not that meetings, coffee, talking, and venting are necessarily bad but that's all some teams do and so nothing concrete is achieved.

57

Focus, then, is vital if the team is to become, and sustain being, high-performing.

58

Focus is influenced by *teamgeist*—the atmosphere in which the work is done shaped by **processes** for communication and collaboration.

59

Many teams fail,
pulled apart by
confusion and
unresolved conflict,
because they (or their
leaders) don't want to
bother with process.

60

Process recognizes teams are about people, not machines. Members need time to get to know each other, and learn how to contribute.

61

Team processes help to inspire, regulate and keep the team on track. A team's energy is a changing dynamic you ignore at your peril.

62

Team processes break down barriers or destroyers of mutual respect, trust, understanding, cooperation and accomplishment in teams.

63

Just like a recipe tells you the time, temperature and method, process informs team members how decisions are made and problems are solved.

64

A team's ROI requires laying a solid foundation: paying attention to process to unleash the full energy of the team for the task.

65

Many leaders struggle because they either do not understand (or pay attention to) team process or task focus. As a result, teams fail.

66

A good team leader is one who recognizes s/he has as much to learn from the team as it needs leadership: the relationship is symbiotic.

67

Leading teams effectively is a calling: without this we will be disappointed with ourselves and frustrated with the results.

Section IV
Leading Teams

Good teams are rooted in clear expectations of deliverables, with well-articulated ways of working together. Members' roles need alignment with top-level goals and the leader steers the ship, supporting team members and ensuring that they contribute their best to the team's effort.

68

Teamwork is not only about bonding, trust-fall exercises and rope courses. Teams need caring leadership and discipline.

69

Teamwork involves leadership to harness the power of a team and *discipline* around working well together to achieve performance goals.

70

Leadership is a needed catalyst for high performing teamwork: without it, many teams fail.

71

Leading a team starts with intentionality: knowing change is needed and determination to mix the ingredients of a team in the right way.

72

'Right way' means expecting team members to work together supportively, holding each other accountable for achieving the common goal.

73

Assembling a team and defining goals is one thing. Pointing the team to work effectively together requires sensitivity, not ego.

74

Leading a team well is about providing a team the time and resources to build a solid bridge from the stated mission to execution.

75

A good leader helps the team to identify its goals, objectives and action plans with clear accountability, rewards and consequences.

76

After defining the
mission and make-up
of a team, leadership
plays another key
role: prodding the
team to shape its
distinct atmosphere.

77

The atmosphere influences how a team works together. Or not. Leaders must allow teams an engagement period just as to-be-married couples need!

78

Leaders must give a team time
to discover its strengths and
diversity: the team needs to fly in
formation, not hit a brick wall.

79

What a leader says and does, and
the time s/he puts into supporting
the team, is an important influence
on a team's ultimate success.

80

Having candid conversations matter. Good leaders steer the team to adopting 'rules of the road' to get to the desired destination in one piece.

81

The wise leader sets the tone for what is expected of a team through purposeful and candid dialogue around task, dynamics *and* process.

82

Prenuptials are important with teams: norms and values need adopting just as if team members were entering into a fantastic marriage.

83

Early team meetings must focus on clarifying purpose, approach and expectations. This takes time because not everyone thinks alike.

84

Conversations need to bring to the surface the diversity in the team so the team engine can rev up using its full wealth of skills.

85

Everyone needs to watch out
for the Team *Twisters* that can
quickly derail the best of teams.
Leaders cannot shun these.

86

Team *Twisters* are hurdles, including
Toxins, **W**hiners, **I**dlers, **S**aboteurs,
Tramplers, **E**gotists and **R**anters who
suck the energy out of teams.

87

Team *Twisters* need to be dealt with promptly or else the whole team will suffer: unfortunately too many leaders look away.

88

Your insurance against these Team *Twisters'* behaviors includes strong leadership and developing team agreements or protocols.

89

Just as you need to decide the shape of your cake (round, square, etc.) you need to establish parameters for shaping how the team will work.

90

Leaders are responsible for helping the team get on its way and to then step aside to leave to the team to do its thing: to grow and blossom.

91

Leaders have to let go to allow the team to evolve, knowing failure is still possible: the team needs to meet its responsibilities.

92

Too many teams look to their leader as the sole source of authority without tapping the collective wisdom to achieve something significant.

93

Leadership *in* the team is a shared responsibility. Members must attend to the task as well as to *the way* the task is being accomplished.

94

Action reviews (plan, do, review and adjust) support continual learning and improvement that benefit the team and the individuals in it.

95

The team's leader has an extra load to bear: to frequently take stock of how the team is doing vis-à-vis mission *and* teamwork.

96

Warning! Just as we each have blind spots, teams and leaders can have blind spots, too. Know when help is needed to get the team back on track.

98

Teamwork is an important phenomenon spoken about too loosely and glibly by leaders and organizations who need to know better.

97

Team support may seem costly until you consider common team failures: lousy delivery, unsolved conflict, silo-work, turnover or burn-out.

99

Leadership is not simply about individual achievement: today's leaders need to provide a steady helm in support of teamwork.

100

Leading effective teams is a priority these days: teams are vital, calling for awareness of what motivates people to work well together.

101

Leading teams
effectively takes time,
communication, care
and foresight: it is
through teamwork that
leaders truly achieve.

Section V
Team Conflict, Camaraderie and Personality

Team camaraderie helps to create connections and relationships and builds among its members an appreciation of the team's diversity. Ensuring that team members find time to get to know each other can pay huge dividends: all work and no play is not the wisest use of time!

102

Many business leaders erroneously believe that simply hiring smart people and paying them well will always make for a great team.

103

Smart people do not always make good team players. Think egomaniacs, lone wolves and people with high intellectual but low emotional IQ!

104

While teams need diversity to excel, it is diversity that tests any team: individual styles and personalities make conflict a given.

105

Teams have introverts and those who love to party. Some who embrace details, others the big picture: if only they understood each other!

106

Bottom line—teams
are complex because
people are different and
use different words to
say the same things.

107

Conflict can undermine a team's ability to work agreeably and productively together while also offering opportunities to build wisdom.

108

I am a better person for having been on teams: I have learned a lot from those with opposite personalities and opposing viewpoints.

109

No vision is too audacious if a highly-diverse team works well: the richness can be awesome—as well as awe-inspiring.

110

Teams blossom from awareness of personality (and other) differences, and how these can play out. Healthy curiosity builds awareness.

111

Without self awareness, teams suffer lost time, personal attacks, low motivation, avoidance of critical issues and mission failure.

112

High performing teams embrace healthy conflict by listening and learning from each other to improve the team's overall productivity.

113

Great teams avoid *toxic* conflict by pitching in together to ensure the team becomes—and acts—as a "we," and not as a "them vs. us."

114

Conflict Lesson 1: Connect different people to clear roles so the team can work at its best: timely mission-delivery without a divorce.

115

Conflict Lesson 2: Listen to other team members with both ears and a big HEART: no one person has all the answers or all the brain power.

116

Conflict Lesson 3: Allow time for individual and team reflection, giving and receiving feedback so everyone and the team can do better next time.

117

The world would be better if the lessons of team conflict were known. Teamwork offers the opportunity to learn before it's too late.

118

If a team overcomes unhealthy conflict—unresolved rows that drain everyone's energy—its power can become a force for greatness.

119

Overcoming adversity opens up new possibilities for a team: it's likely to courageously open new doors and exceed expectations.

120

Managing conflict well in a team can lead to friendship and connection (though I'm not advocating the David Letterman kind!).

121

Top-performing teams enjoy camaraderie attained when diverse attitudes and behaviors are proactively discovered, tapped and *appreciated*.

122

Team camaraderie can be highly motivating, supporting real collaboration, innovation and creativity, and ambitious standards of delivery.

123

Teams create enduring relationships that matter. Camaraderie is the gift of teamwork, spurring learning, innovation and productivity.

124

I firmly believe that no vision or mission is too audacious for a team that is led well and knows what it takes to work well together.

125

Teams work well when they have the right ingredients and enjoy a dynamic that supports members contributing to the best of their ability.

126

Leaders must avoid overly focusing on goals without commensurate attention to the climate they create for high-performing teamwork.

127

Most organizations focus on the individual, providing little guidance on effective teamwork. This must change: less HR and more TeamR!

128

Challenges and opportunities ahead of us will most likely be met, not by the courage of the single 'hero leader' but by heroic teamwork.

129

Leaders have ideas. Teams make change happen.

130

Teamwork provides individuals and leaders opportunities to improve the world and, in so doing, become better persons.

131

Organizations and leaders must re-think teams and teamwork. The old story about teams needs to give way to brilliant, inspiring teamwork.

132

Teams can address tough challenges, in turn building individual resilience in a turbulent world and enhancing our capacity for future challenges.

133

In teams the toughest issues and feelings can be aired and conclusions drawn, resulting in far fewer assumptions and misunderstandings.

134

Effective leadership, clear roles and a compelling purpose are just a start. Teamwork calls for good stewardship of time and resources.

135

A team needs good health: fitness to stay disciplined and focused and good habits to work well together.

136

Like other habits, teams need diligently to balance task with process: a rule of thumb is a 70:30 split between the two; it will pay off.

137

Leaders have a special duty to support teams with a keen awareness of the gnawing gap between mediocre and great teamwork.

138

Leaders and teams need to come together, stay the course and discover from each other what kinds of success are possible.

139

Whatever one's experience of teams, there's always more to learn: we can't take them for granted if we accept they're real game changers.

140

Your insights, reader, are important: see if you can share them like I have shared mine. I believe the conversation is long overdue.

About the Author

Caroline G. Nicholl is Founder and CEO of Blue Apricot Solutions Corporation, offering individual and team coaching, group facilitation, organizational assessment and change management. Caroline was born in London, U.K., and studied law at Bristol University. She joined London's Metropolitan Police (where she worked on changing the force to a service) and served as Chief of Police for the city of Milton Keynes where her pioneering work in restorative justice led to national legislation. Caroline won a year-long Harkness Fellowship that brought her to the United States in 1995. She worked for the Metropolitan Police in Washington D.C. for three years before establishing her consulting practice in 2002. In addition to her consulting work, Caroline is a Chair of two chief executive groups for Vistage International Inc. and an adjunct faculty member for the University of Georgetown's Organizational Development Program. She lives in Alexandria, Virginia.

Caroline can be reached at cnicholl@blueapricotsolutions.com. She can also be found on twitter and via her blog as follows:

 @CarolineNicholl

www.blueapricotsolutions.com/blog

Other Books in the THINKaha Series

The THINKaha book series is for thinking adults who lack the time or desire to read long books, but want to improve themselves with knowledge of the most up-to-date subjects. THINKaha is a leader in timely, cutting-edge books and mobile applications from relevant experts that provide valuable information in a fun, Twitter-brief format for a fast-paced world.

They are available online at http://thinkaha.com or at other online and physical bookstores.

1. *#BOOK TITLE tweet Book01*: 140 Bite-Sized Ideas for Compelling Article, Book, and Event Titles by Roger C. Parker

2. *#DEATHtweet Book01*: A Well Lived Life through 140 Perspectives on Death and its Teachings by Timothy Tosta

3. *#DIVERSITYtweet Book01*: Embracing the Growing Diversity in Our World by Deepika Bajaj

4. *#DREAMtweet Book01*: Inspirational Nuggets of Wisdom from a Rock and Roll Guru to Help You Live Your Dreams by Joe Heuer

5. *#ENTRYLEVELtweet Book01*: Taking Your Career from Classroom to Cubicle by Heather R. Huhman

6. *#JOBSEARCHtweet Book01*: 140 job search nuggets for managing your career and landing your dream job by Barbara Safani

7. *#LEADERSHIPtweet Book01*: 140 bite-sized ideas to help you become the leader you were born to be by Kevin Eikenberry

8. *#MILLENNIALtweet Book01*: 140 Bite-sized Ideas for Managing the Millennials by Alexandra Levit

9. *#MOJOtweet*: 140 Bite-Sized Ideas on How to Get and Keep Your Mojo by Marshall Goldsmith

10. *#PARTNER tweet Book01*: 140 Bite-Sized Ideas for Succeeding in Your Partnerships by Chaitra Vedullapalli

11. *#PROJECT MANAGEMENT tweet Book01*: 140 Powerful Bite-Sized Insights on Managing Projects by Guy Ralfe and Himanshu Jhamb

12. *#QUALITYtweet Book01*: 140 Bite-Sized Ideas to Deliver Quality in Every Project by Tanmay Vora

13. *#SOCIALMEDIA NONPROFIT tweet Book01*: 140 Bite-Sized Ideas for Nonprofit Social Media Engagement by Janet Fouts with Beth Kanter

14. *#SPORTS tweet Book01*: What I Learned from Coaches About Sports and Life by Ronnie Lott with Keith Potter

15. *#THINKtweet Book01*: Bite-sized lessons for a fast paced world by Rajesh Setty